$$a^m \times a^n = a^{m+n}$$

$$\frac{1}{3} + \frac{2}{3}$$

$$4\overline{)624}$$

"Mathematics, in a sense, is logic
let loose in the field of the imagination."
—Margaret Wertheim

$$R = P\frac{\ell}{S}$$

$$a^2 + b^2 = c^2$$

For Mike & Leo

Special thanks to Erich Patrick Enke
for being so wonderfully knowledgeable, helpful, & patient.
And to Elena, Dmitri, Seraphima, Johannes, & Serena
for sharing Erich's smarts with me.
(He made me excited about math! Is he some sort of wizard?)

VIKING

An imprint of Penguin Random House LLC, New York

First published in the United States of America by Viking, an imprint of Penguin Random House LLC, 2019

Visit us online at penguinrandomhouse.com

LIBRARY OF CONGRESS CATALOGING-IN-PUBLICATION DATA IS AVAILABLE
ISBN 9780451480903

Manufactured in China

9   10

The artwork in this book was created using Higgins inks on paper, Photoshop CC (I heart Kyle Brushes),
and Rebelle 3. The main text was lettered with hand-carved bamboo calligraphy pens (that I bought
on the street outside Shanghai) and ink. Soundtrack provided by OmWriter.

I'M TRYING to LOVE MATH

WORDS & PICTURES by bethany bARTon

VIKING

IF YOU ASK ME, MATH IS NOT VERY LOVABLE.

A SPACE ALIEN?
WHAT DO <u>YOU</u> KNOW ABOUT MATH?

Well, math is **understood** all over the earth, no matter what language people speak.

5 + 12 = 17

Scientists took examples of life on Earth—things like language, music, and math—and put them onto golden records.

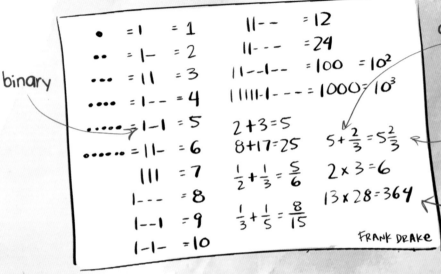

binary

FRANK DRAKE

addition

fractions

multiplication

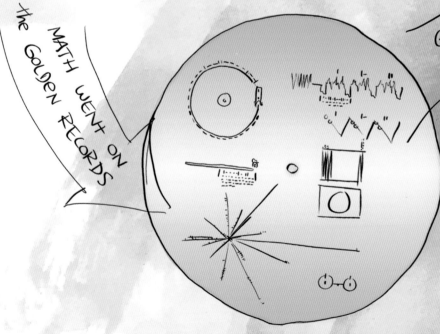

MATH WENT ON the GOLDEN RECORDS

GOLDEN RECORDS WENT ABOARD VOYAGER SPACECRAFTS

The golden records went on space probes they sent into deep space— for curious aliens like me to find!

Let's see, I just need...

🍺 + 🍺 + 🍺 $2\frac{1}{2}$ CUPS + FLOUR

🍺 + 🍺   3/4 CUP SUGAR + 3/4 CUP BROWN SUGAR

+ 1 CUP BUTTER

BUTTER
NET WEIGHT 4 OZ (113g)
¼ CUP   ½ CUP
TABLESPOONS
1 2 3 4 5 6 7 8

HMM...LOOKS LIKE I NEED 2 OF THESE to EQUAL A CUP...

WAIT.

BAKING IS JUST A
BUNCH OF MATH, ISN'T IT?

(whoA.)

IN FACT, THIS WHOLE RECIPE
IS BASICALLY A WORD PROBLEM!

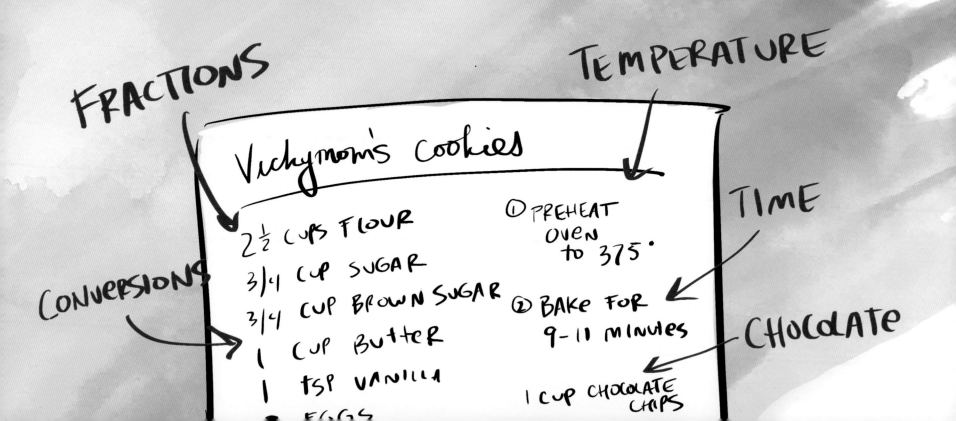

FRACTIONS

TEMPERATURE

CONVERSIONS

TIME

CHOCOLATE

Vickymom's cookies

2½ CUPS FLOUR
3/4 CUP SUGAR
3/4 CUP BROWN SUGAR
1 CUP Butter
1 tsp VANILLA
EGGS

① PREHEAT
OVEN
to 375°

② BAKE FOR
9-11 minutes

1 CUP CHOCOLATE
CHIPS

OKAY, YOU SEE THIS
MATH PROBLEM HERE?

785
X5
———

I AM GOING TO
TRY TO LOVE It!

(MAYBE IF I STARE AT It...
AND THINK ABOUT COOKIES...)

785
x5
_____

Nope, I'm ALREADY BORED.

WHAT IF I JAZZ IT UP WITH SOME EXTRA NUMBERS?

$$8910 \quad \begin{array}{r} 785 \\ \times 5 \end{array} \quad (6 \div 12)$$

$$0000.16$$

$$16\overline{)a+b}$$

AND ADD SOME OF THESE SYMBOLS...

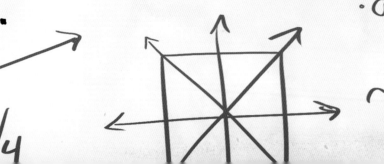

$$\frac{9}{100} = .09$$

$$^1/_4$$

WHOOPS.

You got a little carried away.
PARALLEL
PERPENDICULAR
INTERSECTING
HOLD HERE to SHAKE
HOLD HERE to SHAKE
HOLD HERE to SHAKE
2+3=5
0.98=.98
.000009001

$(ab)^n = a^n b^n$

$A = \frac{\div}{2} bh$

089I
263

3.1415

THIS IS WAY TOO MUCH MATH.
CAN WE SHAKE THE BOOK AND
MAKE SOME NUMBERS FALL OUT?

89I0785 $(6 \div 12)$

$\frac{2}{3} \times \frac{1}{3} = 1$

x50000 I6

$= 24$

$16\sqrt{a+b}$

2^{12}

6×4

JUST HOLD IT TIGHT AND
GIVE IT A FEW GOOD SHAKES.

HOLD HERE to SHAKE

HOLD HERE to SHAKE

HOLD HERE to SHAKE

$\frac{1}{100}$

.09

$\pi = 3.14$

69% OF x

$9 \times 2 = 18$

.69x

1/4

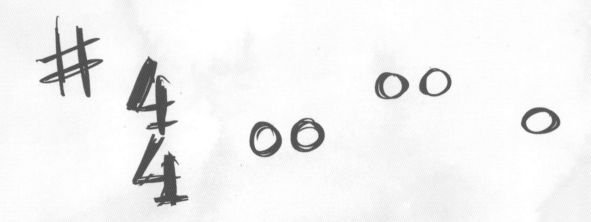

WHEW! THANKS!

MATH IS JUST SO BORING...
It's NOT LIKE YOU CAN DANCE to IT.

Math is also about exploring! About finding new ways to get places, and helping you find your way back.

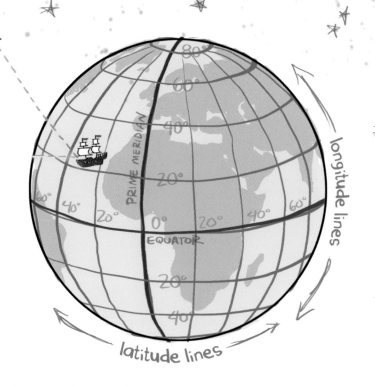

For centuries, sailors navigated using the stars, special measuring tools, and lots of math!

(chronometer)

(sextant)

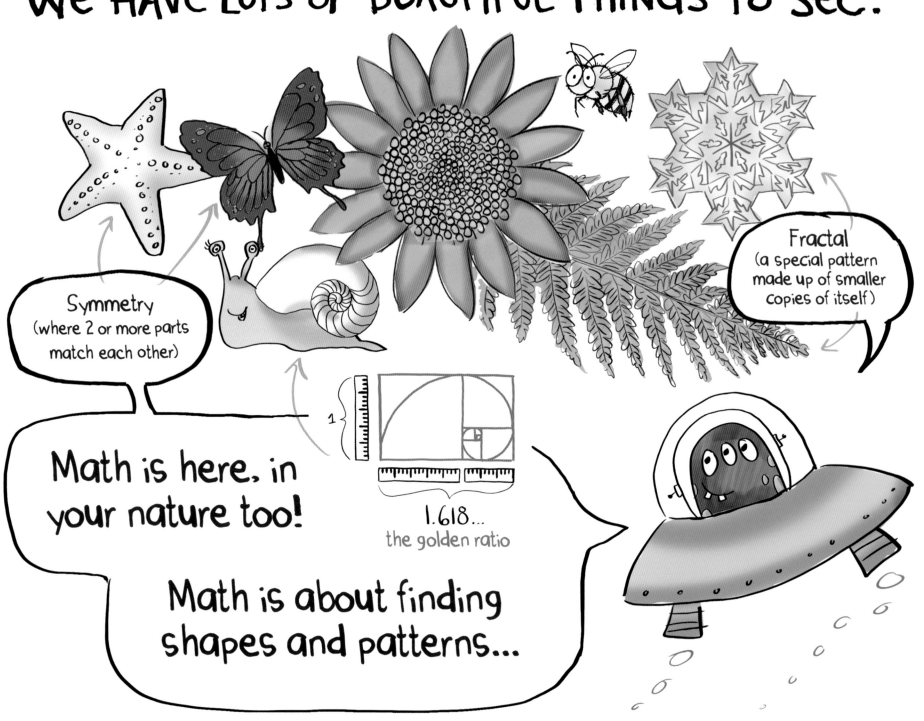

OH NO YOU DON'T!

YOU'RE MAKING IT ALL ABOUT MATH AGAIN!
BUT IT'S MY TURN TO TEACH YOU SOMETHING.

INTRODUCING
EARTH'S GREATEST
INVENTION:

PIZZA.

Pi represents a number. It's a super long number, so you usually shorten it to 3.14.

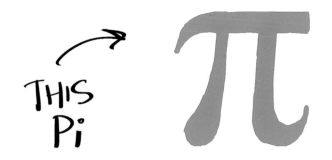

THIS
Pi

π

NOT THIS
Pie

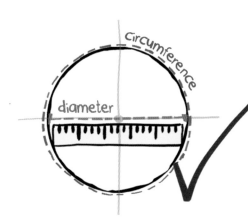

It's a sort of cheat code to figure out the size of a circle.

π x diameter = circumference

Pi is also what's called an irrational number, which means it goes on forever and never repeats!

Like this!

π = 3.141592653358979

WELL, THAT WAS UNEXPECTED.

I NEVER THOUGHT I'D
SAY THIS... BUT THIS IS
TOO MUCH PI FOR ME.

HOLD HERE to SHAKE

HOLD HERE to SHAKE

HOLD HERE to SHAKE

HOLD HERE to SHAKE

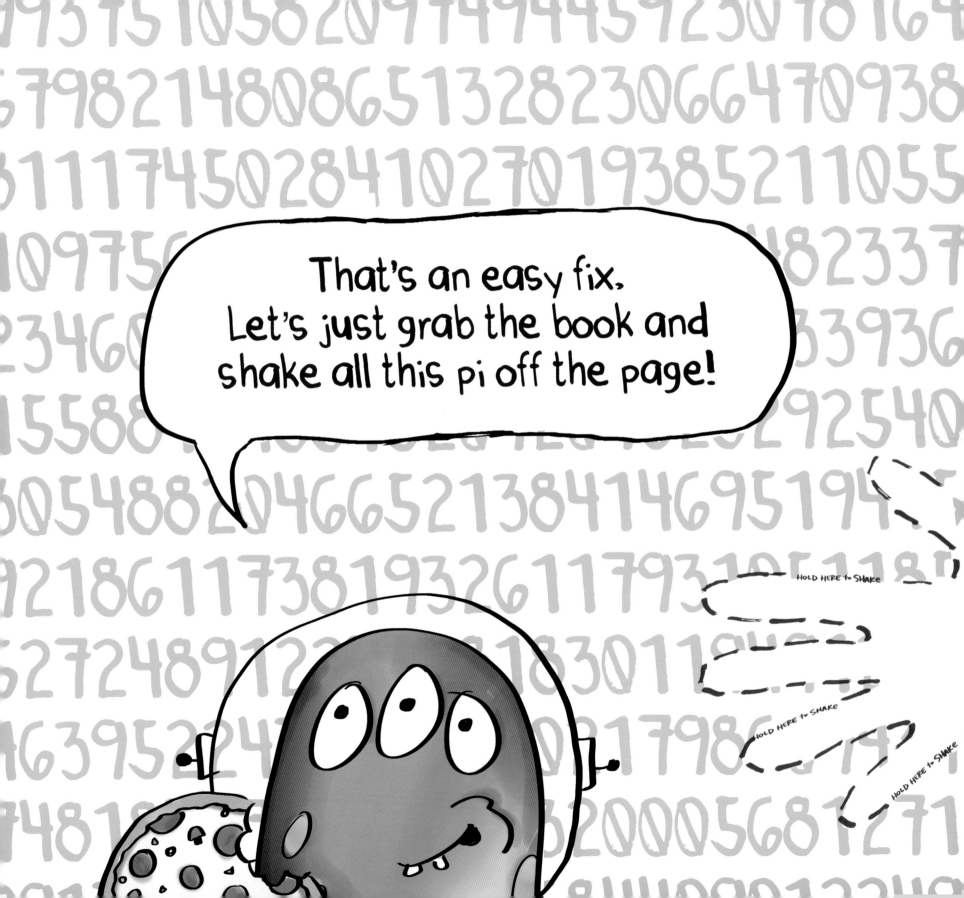

WHEW! THAT'S BETTER.

I'LL ADMIT, SOME OF THIS MATH STUFF IS COOL.

BUT MATH CAN STILL BE PRETTY FRUSTRATING...

LIKE HOW THERE'S ONLY ONE RIGHT ANSWER!

I'm okay!

That's true...

but it's also what makes math so helpful!
Math gives us a set of rules everyone can agree on.

So we know how far
to travel to get places,

— 10 MILES —

how fast we're
moving on our way,

and how much things
cost when we get there.

YOU KNOW, MATH IS A PART OF SO MANY THINGS I ALREADY LOVE...

I GUESS I DON'T NEED TO <u>TRY</u> TO LOVE IT AT ALL.

It TURNS OUT... I ALREADY DO.

Planet Homework!

YIKes.

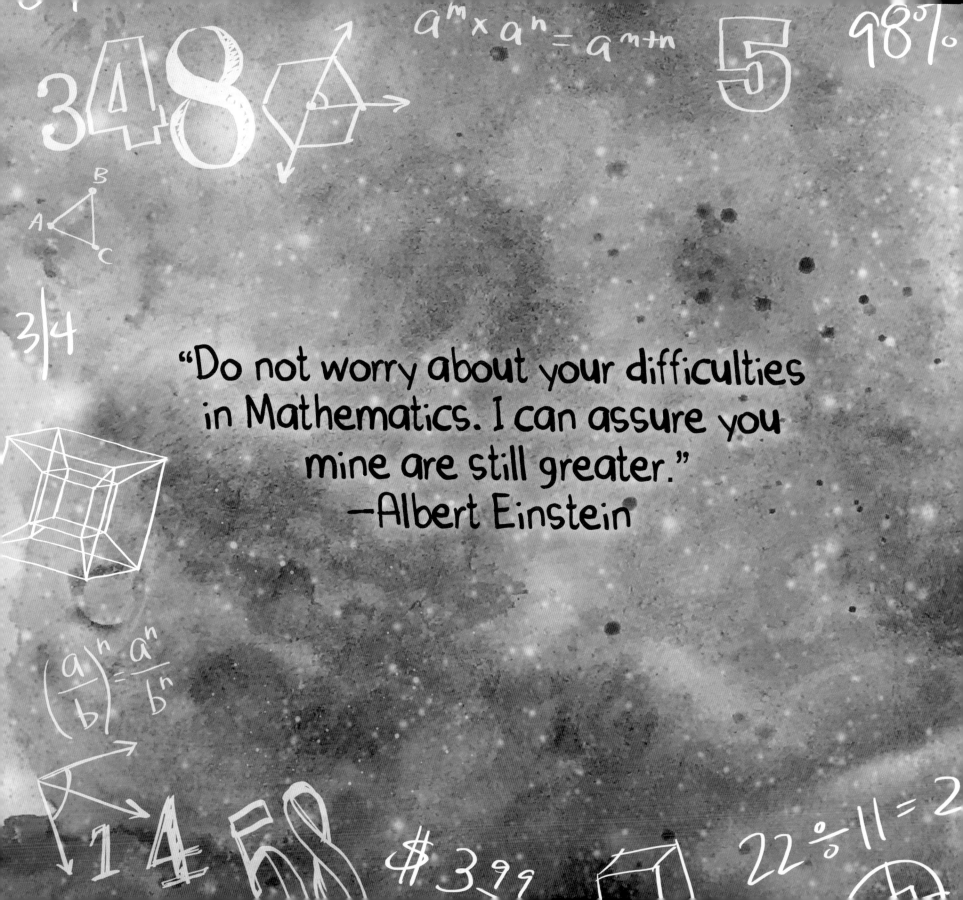